Learn a Wicked

Awesome Boston

Accent

by Ivan Borodin

ISBN-13: 978-1490345994
ISBN-10: 149034599X

Introduction

Actors occasionally have a tough time at auditions. If an attempt at an accent goes wrong, they usually don't want to even talk about it, much less relive it. With all the misconceptions about acting floating about, putting on an accent seems to take on an air of mysticism.

When it comes to learning accents, science beats out magic. The way to learn a Boston accent is to make your way through this program, allowing your mind and voice to digest the subtle vowel and consonant changes.

The Boston accent has experienced a new life in cinema as of late, with audiences appreciating the irresistible honesty and poetry of the dialect.

I am humbled by the opportunity to share its secrets with you. It warms me to the core to bring you the tools you'll need to pull off a wicked awesome Boston accent.

1

The Short O leans toward AW

This change is a tremendous red flag that the speaker is from New England.

Throughout this manual, this change will be annotated with **aw** written above it.

   aw   aw   aw   aw
bomb, bother, Rhonda, God

            aw   aw
There's *not* a whole *lot* of experience with those three.

               aw
We found his *body* by the airport.

      aw
Even *vodka* has its limitations.

2

Consider this vowel change your defense against sounding like you're from New York. New York and Massachusetts border each other, so it's only naturally that the accents would contain similarities. New Yorker generally pronounce the short O, but people from Boston almost universally change it to AW.

                                               aw

I certainly agree with both of my *colleagues.*

                                            aw

Did you think you'd waltz out of here *scot-free?*

             aw   aw

We've *got* ourselves a *monster.*

              aw   aw

Do you *honestly* think he can eliminate our *problem?*

     aw   aw

Thomas didn't wait for a *response.*

3

aw   aw

This summer is the *hottest* one on record, and that's *not* a good thing.

The sun is playing hide and seek with a *flock* of clouds.

Jonathan parked his *Honda* sideways, effectively *blocking* in everyone.

4

5

AW leans toward the short O

In what amounts to an inversion of the last vowel change,

these two sounds seem to blend.

small, long, all, off, always, call, lawsuits

He's able to stand *tall* amid this mess.

I risk *falling* from grace if I pursue this further.

The agent kept *walking*.

Drink your *coffee* and pretend you're happy to be married to me.

The *brawling* originated from a few snappy insults.

That *fall almost* broke my back.

6

I've *lost* my nerve more than once.

Paul was *already* past the pool.

7

AR turns to AH

This R-drop is accompanied with a slight rise in pitch on stressed syllables.

parks, starts, party, bartender, guitar

                                                   aw

This is going to be a *hard* pill to swallow.

Look how it gets *dark* down there.

The rusty old *cart* was underwater.

I've fallen *farther* than you could understand.

                                                   aw

There was a *faraway* look in his eyes as he contemplated the back wall of the *bar*.

8

Close, but no *cigar*.

I'm telling you the truth, *Sarge*.

                          aw
I am in *charge* of the operation.

9

The Long U thickens

Place a slight 'uh' before the long U. When the word is stressed, there is also the tendency to rise in pitch.

suit, shoots, cool, pool, food, Jacuzzi

She is interested in things that I *do*.

I'll arrest *you* right now.

I just went *through* that.

Take *two* and call me in the morning.

Remove your *shoes*.

           aw
There was a lot of *loose* talk.

The least I can *do* is give you the *scoop* in person.

10

Scientists always *knew* just a little more than they cared to share.

I didn't count on swimming *through* an entire *school* of jellyfish.

I handpicked this *group*.

11

Stressed R-endings reduce and rise in pitch

To portray yourself as a speaker from Boston, be sure to milk this dramatic change.

there, years, awareness, nearly

aw

George and *Morgan* are not *normally* ironic men.

The sound of laughter was *born* on the night wind.

Boston's many *firsts* include the United States' *first* public school and *first* subway system.

If you don't open this *door*, I'm breaking it down.

aw

We had two *hours* to chop it up.

12

Sweat began to drip from my *hair*.

aw

His father *worked* in a coal mine.

13

The Short I darkens

This sound is pronounced very clearly in standard American English, but takes on a rougher edge in Boston.

little, big, killed, figure, winter, spring

Listen, I *think* someone has been tampering without *permission.*

Jimmy isn't exactly what you'd call a *physical* player.

There was *blistering* chemistry between *Christy* and myself.

I'm trying to *pinpoint* why you seem *familiar.*

Her eyes were *fixed* on the ground.

In *typical* Boston fashion, you wouldn't know anything was going on.

14

His *fingernails* were lined with yellow streaks.

It was no time to *split* hairs.

15

The Long E darkens

In the standard American accent, the long E is crystal clear. The speaker from Boston changes the vowel by coloring it with a U sound.

scream, even, weakest, demon, freak

I *feel* that one should let go of nicknames by the age of thirty.

Do you recognize *either* of them?

aw

Get ready to tear into its *weak* spots.

He's the one who put you to *sleep.*

What do you think your *teammates* are about to do to *me*?

16

I'm *reading* a book about *free* trade.

That was something *we* weren't supposed to *see*.

Keep in mind what you taught me about taking a *beating*.

I *need* to work.

Either Steven didn't *eat* right, or nobody ever taught him about personal hygeine.

17

The Long A darkens

name, April, change, safe, fascination

When it comes to *playing* basketball, talking trash is part of the *game.*

If you see me in a fight with a bear, *pray* for the bear.

That's a clever *rationalization* you *came* up with.

This is exactly the right *place.*

Get me *information* on the people who were with you last night.

The broad-shouldered figure wore a helmet with an *opaque face* shield.

Where can I buy an industrial-strength cheese *grater?*

18

aw

I cannot allow you to jeopardize an ongoing *investigation*.

Okay, then just *say* that.

19

The Short U opens up to 'ah'

judge, result, bug, other, must, fun, stun

I get into relationships with people who could never meet my standards, then *punish* them for being who they are.

      aw

A Bobble-head *sculpture* stands sentry outside the gift store.

Show business is made of stairs, and there are those who go *up* and those who go down.

You're *gonna love* this guy.

I can live without seeing the lady who *dumped* me.

It *doesn't* take a genius to tell where the *trouble* is *coming* from.

I know a thing or two about *muscle* memory.

20

The *butterfly* landed on the petals of the tiger lily.

aw

He knew the cop couldn't be *trusted*.

Take a moment to attempt the following passage, an excerpt from the horror novel *Pandora 2013: Hullabaloo*. In this brief monologue, Sebastian attempts to talk a tourist into leaving the cursed shopping center before things turn ugly.

22

Passage #1 - Sebastian's plea

I could do a lot of things to make a living. There are two video stores left on the Grand Strand. During the summer, restaurants hire waiters by the busload. That real estate office just across from Pandora Tours is run by a guy who drinks at the Hornet's Nest. I have a standing offer to work either reception or to open my own desk. I'm not even above cleaning toilets.

So why do I give tours? This business is not for the faint of heart, and this job puts me in a position to help you clowns avoid shooting yourselves in the foot.

Consider some of the changes you could make to affect a Boston accent:

The Short O becomes AW

aw aw aw
lot, not, job

       aw

I could do a *lot* of things to make a living.

    aw

I'm *not* even above cleaning toilets.

       aw

This business is *not* for the faint of heart, and this *job* puts me in a position to help you clowns avoid shooting yourselves in the foot.

The Short U opens up

summer, busload, just, run

During the *summer*, restaurants hire waiters by the *busload*.

That real estate office *just* across from Pandora Tours is *run* by a guy who drinks at the Hornet's Nest.

The Long U darkens

do, two, shooting

       aw

I could *do* a lot of things to make a living.

There are *two* video stores left on the Grand Strand.

       aw

This business is not for the faint of heart, and this job puts me in a position to help you clowns avoid *shooting* yourselves in the foot.

AW becomes a Short O

office, across, offer

That real estate *office* just *across* from Pandora Tours is run by a guy who drinks at the Hornet's Nest.

I have a standing *offer* to work either reception or to open my own desk.

Drop R endings and rise in pitch

stores, during, hire, work, hornet, tours

There are two video *stores* left on the Grand Strand.

During the summer, restaurants *hire* waiters by the busload.

That real estate office just across from Pandora Tours is run by a guy who drinks at the *Hornet's* Nest.

I have a standing offer to *work* either reception or to open my own desk.

So why do I give *tours*?

Take a final pass at the monologue, attempting to retain some of the vowel and consonant changes.

29

Sebastian's plea (changes in italics):

aw

I could *do* a *lot* of things to make a living. There are *two*

video *stores* left on the Grand Strand. *During* the

summer, restaurants *hire* waiters by the *busload*. That

real estate *office just across* from Pandora Tours is *run*

by a guy who drinks at the *Hornet's* Nest. I have a

standing *offer* to *work* either reception or to open my own

aw

desk. I'm *not* even above cleaning toilets.

30

aw

So why do I give *tours*? This business is *not* for the faint

aw

of heart, and this *job* puts me in a position to help you

clowns avoid *shooting* yourselves in the foot.

Attempt the following passage in your most wicked Boston accent. Taken from *Pandora 2013: Hullabaloo*, this monologue features Clarence Gifford, an older deputy. In this speech, Clarence tries to reason out a situation with a younger man by using a metaphor.

Passage #2: Clarence's metaphor

I'll share a cautionary tale with you. A regular guy survives a shipwreck and is marooned on a desert island with a world-famous supermodel. As you would imagine, the mismatched pair become an item.

After a while, the guy grows tired of it. He asks his supermodel girlfriend to dress up as a man, put on a moustache, and meet him on the other side of the island. She obliges him, and when they meet, the guy doesn't break into kinky relations. Instead, he sits her down and spends an evening bragging about his girl.

Sometimes we make love to a woman, but more often we make love to the story they inspire in us. We get wrapped up in the plot of our life.

34

Consider the changes you could make to affect a Boston accent:

Drop R endings and rise in pitch

share, world, pair, tired, girl, more, inspire

I'll *share* a cautionary tale with you.

A regular guy survives a shipwreck and is marooned on a desert island with a *world*-famous supermodel.

As you would imagine, the mismatched *pair* become an item.

After a while, the guy grows *tired* of it.

He asks his supermodel *girl*friend to dress up as a man.

Sometimes we make love to a woman, but *more* often we make love to the story they *inspire* in us.

35

The Short U opens up

become, up, other, doesn't, sometimes, love

As you would imagine, the mismatched pair *become* an item.

He asks his supermodel girlfriend to dress *up* as a man, put on a moustache, and meet him on the *other* side of the island.

She obliges him, and when they meet, the guy *doesn't* break into kinky relations.

Sometimes we make *love* to a woman, but more often we make *love* to the story they inspire in *us*.

aw

We get wrapped *up* in the plot of our life.

The Short I darkens

ship, mismatched, into, kinky, sits, in

A regular guy survives a *ship*wreck and is marooned on a desert island with a world-famous supermodel.

As you would imagine, the *mismatched* pair become an item.

She obliges him, and when they meet, the guy doesn't break *into kinky* relations.

Instead, he *sits* her down and spends an evening bragging about his girl.

aw

We get wrapped up *in* the plot of our life.

Take another swing at the monologue, attempting to

retain some of the vowel and consonant changes.

Clarence's metaphor (changes in italics):

I'll *share* a cautionary tale with you. A regular guy survives a *ship*wreck and is marooned on a desert island with a *world*-famous supermodel. As you would imagine, the *mismatched pair become* an item.

After a while, the guy grows *tired* of it. He asks his supermodel *girlfriend* to dress *up* as a man, put on a moustache, and meet him on the *other* side of the island. She obliges him, and when they meet, the guy *doesn't* break *into kinky* relations. Instead, he *sits* her down and spends an evening bragging about his girl.

Sometimes we make *love* to a woman, but *more* often we make *love* to the story they *inspire* in us. We get wrapped

aw

up in the plot of our life.

38

Take a stab at the following passage in your most wicked awesome Boston accent. It is an excerpt from *Pandora 2013: Hullabaloo*. Isaac, a mysterious and potentially dangerous stranger, introduces himself to a lost visitor.

Passage #3: Isaac's Eccentric Introduction

Tonight is one of those nights wherein the laws of nature contradict themselves. This mall is bordered by a forest and a bog. The air should howl with wildlife, yet even the cicadas dare not cry out. But somewhere in the spaces between heartbeats, if you cock an ear, you'll detect the plaintive* demand for answers, a whisper crafted from a soul in need.

*plaintive–a plaintive sound is high and sad, like someone crying. Example: The plaintive cry of wolves.

Consider the changes you could make to affect a Boston accent:

The Short O becomes AW

aw   aw   aw

contradict, bog, not

Tonight is one of those nights wherein the laws of nature *contradict* themselves.

                                            aw

This mall is bordered by a forest and a *bog*.

The air should howl with wildlife, yet even the cicadas dare *not* cry out.

41

Drop R endings and rise in pitch

bordered, forest, air, dare, heartbeats, ear

                                                        aw
This mall is *bordered* by a *forest* and a bog.

The *air* should howl with wildlife, yet even the cicadas *dare* not cry out.

But somewhere in the spaces between *heartbeats*, if you cock an *ear*, you'll detect the plaintive demand for answers, a whisper crafted from a soul in need.

42

The Long A darkens

nature, spaces, plaintive

Tonight is one of those nights wherein the laws of *nature* contradict themselves.

But somewhere in the *spaces* between heartbeats, if you cock an ear, you'll detect the *plaintive* demand for answers, a whisper crafted from a soul in need.

Take another swing at the monologue, attempting to retain some of the vowel and consonant changes.

43

Isaac's Introduction (changes in italics)

Tonight is one of those nights wherein the laws of *nature*

aw

contradict themselves. This mall is *bordered* by a *forest*

aw

and a *bog*. The *air* should howl with wildlife, yet even

aw

the cicadas *dare not* cry out. But somewhere in the

aw

spaces between *heartbeats*, if you cock an *ear*, you'll
detect the *plaintive* demand for answers, a whisper
crafted from a soul in need.

Bonus Lesson #1

This lesson is designed to help you speak with a wicked awesome Boston accent, using key vowel and consonant changes when applied to a text.

Drop R endings

arch, before, convert, farthest, purple

The Short I darkens

different, religion, consider it significant, a living part of our history

The Short U opens up to the Short O

becoming, covered, lumber, just above, one Sunday

The Short O becomes AW

consonant, optimistic, spot, philosophical, clocks, plot, embodies

In the following speech, an optimistic dreamer speaks about the magic of a strange place and his hometown.

Are you asking me what I think about that shopping center? First off, from this seat, if I arch my back a teensy bit, I can see the main building just above the trees. I consider it significant that I can see that from here.

I've lived here since I was a child. Never moved. Went to school locally. The farthest I've strayed is New Hampshire, where I had to attend a medical conference, and I can't say I enjoyed it. You see, even before things changed, I have always sensed a magical presence in our area. Like I said, I haven't travelled, but from what I see on the news and in the media, the world is becoming a rather selfish place. It's all about punching clocks and achieving goals. People see a tree and plot to convert it to lumber. When I look at a pine tree covered in snow, I see a living part of our history. There's magic in that.

I remember when that mall had to be closed down. The carousel came to life one Sunday morning, right? The atrium was overrun with purple horses and orange rhinos. Massachusetts being so steeped in religion, there were whispers about the Devil. I was struck with a different perspective. I mean, what a gift! To have a magical treasure right here in our hometown.

But you want to know how I think that enchanted shopping center works, right? Well, I couldn't presume to say. I can't tell you how a pine tree grows. How could I know about any other magic?

48

49

Final Notes

The author intends to make support for this publication available online. At the time of this writing, YouTube is the most popular site for posting videos that demonstrate chapters of this book.

To find online lessons in the Boston Accent, search **IvanBorodin** and/or **Learn a Wicked Awesome Boston Accent** on YouTube.

The author recognizes the Internet is an evolving beast. Should another site become the leader in social media, please search for support for this book using the tags listed above.

Sources for Future Study

The Departed - This award-winning film features some amazing performances from actors at the peak of their powers. The focus of the movie is not the Boston accent, so there will be spots where the accent takes a back seat to the themes and events. If while reading this manual, you wondered what was meant by "The Short O becomes AW", well, just listen to how nearly everyone in The Departed pronounces the word 'cop'. "I'm nawt a cawp". "You're a cawp."

Film: The Fighter, Mystic River, The Town, Good Will Hunting, Gone Baby Gone, Shutter Island, Black Mass, Spotlight, Manchester by the Sea

Television: Bojack Horseman episode 1.5

About the Author

Learning an accent? Lots of fun. Trying to figure it out without a decent handbook? Not so much.

My years as an instructor of accent reduction gave me perspective on dialects. Their secrets began to reveal themselves. Teaching dialects has been a unique, unexpected detour. I've been blessed with the chance to help countless actors pull off a wide spectrum of accents. Seeing their faces when it all comes together is like drawing a winning lottery ticket.

I've also been fortunate to perform with dialects myself, most notably on two of J.J. Abrams' television shows, *Alias* and *Undercovers*.

Also by Ivan Borodin

Speak with an Accent

Explore the full range of a dozen accents (Australian, French, Russian, Southern, German, British, New York, Scottish, Cockney, Japanese, Arabic and Irish) on this Compact Disc. An absolute must-have for character actors.

Speak with a New York Accent

In the Big Apple, you keep your head down and avoid eye contact with strangers. But when you decide to talk like a New Yawka, you better bring the necessary vowel and consonant changes—and the attitude. Forgetaboutit!

Learn a Southern Drawl

Everyone has their version of a Southern accent, but with this manual, you'll have the one born of pure Dixie charm.

Speak with an African Accent

Maximize your practice time with this concise guide. Key vowel and consonant changes are outlined in a strategic manner, allowing the reader to gain speedy confidence. This handbook serves as an introduction to the pronunciation shifts needed to speak with a convincing African accent.

Speak with an Irish Brogue

St. Patrick's Day comes once a year, but there's always a reason to break into an Irish Brogue. Whether you're an actor required to tinge your voice in emerald bravado, or a barfly hoping to catch the attention of a head-turning blonde, this manual will lead to soaring success.

Learn a Scottish Burr

Finally, the concise manual that every actor needs is here! With easy to follow vowel substitution patterns and mastery drills, you'll benefit from years of experience coaching actors as they create epic accents and dialects.

Speak with a Russian Accent

People love Russian characters. Actors are often called upon to perform with a Russian accent. Good actors love playing Russian characters, because when solid writing matches with clever choices, the results border on magical. Ivan Borodin has done a Russian accent on television shows such as 'Alias' and 'Undercovers' and has taught dialects for decades, finally delivers this concise manual on the Russian accent. Inside you'll find all the advice you'll need on Russian speech, as well as exercises to help you speak with integrity.